# INFINITE
## HEALING

The Metamorphosis of a Grieving Soul

Robin Major-Oliphant

INFINITE HEALING

Edited by Shawn Jackson
Cover Design by Design Place
Published by One2Mpower Publishing LLC

# INFINITE HEALING

*He heals the brokenhearted and binds up their wounds.*

– Psalms 147:3 (NIV)

## Broken Wing

A poem written somewhere between my breaking point and my decision to take control of my healing.

---

*This must be what it feels like to be a broken-winged butterfly.*
*Suffocated, exhausted…*
*Frustrated, and afraid.*
*Nearly lifeless.*
*Suffocating because the air down here is so cold and thick,*
*That breathing no longer comes naturally.*
*Exhausted because no matter how hard you try,*
*You'll never soar to higher heights with a broken wing.*
*Frustrated because you realize your potential,*
*But you can't visualize how to get from broken to mended.*
*Afraid to start over from where you are,*
*To experience metamorphosis in your new season.*

*This must be what it feels like to be a broken-winged butterfly.*
*But this feeling is an illusion.*
*Your emotions have taken the driver's seat,*
*Headed nowhere fast.*

*But wait! There is still hope.*
*Eliminate the illusion.*
*Heal, forgive, and remember.*
*Accept what is, what was, and let it GO!*

# DEDICATION

This book is dedicated to the "strong friend". The friend/family member who is often most revered for their strength and bravery, with no room to find comfort and healing in your own weaknesses.

You are not alone. While it is an honor to be admired for your strength, I encourage you to find comfort and peace in being honest, vulnerable, and intentional in healing through grief and trauma. I know that the people in your world depends on you but, remember YOU need YOU. Take this time to focus on yourself and heal.

# INTRODUCTION

I have fought many battles in my life, some physical, others mental and spiritual. One thing that has proven to be my reality though is that the infinite battle of healing through grief and restoring my soul has been the toughest by far. I'm not sure if this is normal, but I've spent more time obsessing over the proverbial "end" to my grief and not enough time focusing on myself personally. Simply put, I didn't care about the process. I just wanted the pain of it all to end, and in some cases, admittedly, by any means necessary. The cliché scriptures and sermons focused on healing and overcoming, and the prayers and comforting words of encouragement were no longer enough to help me through. I had buried so much hurt through "forgiving and releasing" the good old Christian way, my way, that I failed to truly acknowledge my own feelings, evaluate circumstances, and act accordingly. My flawed thought process of forgiving, extending grace, and moving on left no room for me to truly heal and take the next step toward restoration. Therefore, the core of my foundation had been shattered, yet I continued to try to re-build myself on sinking sand.

Trauma begets grief, and grief often leads to depression if your trauma wounds go unaddressed. This is where I am at the time of writing this, which is new for me because while I often suggest that my clients write for healing, it just hasn't been my thing. If you had told me in January 2018 that I would be here, grieving and trying to find my way back to myself, I would not have believed you. It wasn't until January 2020 that I realized I was grieving something, but I could not put my finger on what it was. It seemed as though I was okay until I realized I wasn't. That revelation was so earth-shattering that instead of digging up the root (trauma) and addressing the grief, I hid from it. I hid from it in an attempt to avoid looking like a fraud! The diagnosis of depression almost always comes with the label of having mental health issues. Mental health issues, to some equate to being "crazy," emotionally unstable, sick, or disabled. Since I had already been through the motions of being clinically depressed, being mandated to see a therapist, and even on medication, there was no way I was willing to give in to the stigma of having mental health issues again. To avoid a second diagnosis and avoid being medicated, I struggled with accepting the fact that I was not okay for nearly twelve months as things continued to spiral out of control. By the time I accepted the fact that I was not okay, two years had passed; 2018 through 2020, and the avalanche of trauma had buried

11

me so deep that I found myself lost, confused, extremely angry, and in a state of bewilderment. How was I okay one day but suffering from depression AGAIN the next?

I'd been completely healed and delivered from depression for over three years! Not only was I healed and delivered, but I also spent the better part of my day over the years healing and delivering others. I was the "strong friend," saving, supporting, healing, and delivering everyone else but me. How is it that now I am the one who needs saving, support, healing, and deliverance? Could it be that I have had everything within me to save others, and yet no true revelation of how to help heal myself? I don't think so. I choose to believe that at this moment, as I am writing this, I'm all poured out. An empty vessel needing to be refilled, supported, and loved on. Regardless of the why, I am ready to focus on the how. One thing I am certain of is the trauma that led me here was not a singular event or occurrence. The grief I am transitioning through consists of a myriad of disappointments, losses, betrayals, and bad choices, which led to terrible emotional outcomes. I'm choosing now to peel back every layer, addressing every aspect of my grief, one layer at a time.

# PART I

# TRANSFORMATION THROUGH GRIEF

# METAMORPHOSIS

Grief is often simply summed up as "deep sorrow," however, there is so much more to it than that. Grief is a spiritual, emotional, and physical trauma response that comes with many different emotions such as sadness, anger, depression, loneliness, denial, and acceptance. While many would not admit it, or may not even recognize it, most of us have dealt with grief to some degree. If I may be honest, I struggled with the fact that I was grieving because labeling my emotional state seemed too close to the Big D—Depression. Because I had struggled with depression in my early twenties, the thought of acknowledging grief was too close to the idea of reclaiming the taboo label of experiencing depression. What I had to come to grips with is the fact that grief is a natural human response to trauma. The difference between whether or not the grief we experience will be to our detriment is how and if we address it.

Let's face it. We've all experienced traumas such as the loss of a loved one, a relationship, pet, career, or even disappointment from failed expectations. We often experience these types of traumas without realizing that our natural and reflexive response consists of many different emotions and feelings associated with the grieving process. Instead of feeling and processing these emotions, we run from them. Praying for the end, numbing through the pain, or spending the bulk of the transition in absolute denial with the cliché audible response, "I am okay," which completely contradicts the emotions we are experiencing internally.

The catalyst to overcoming grief, though, is recognizing and accepting the fact that we are actually experiencing it and realizing that grief is cyclical, and healing is infinite. I am not sure when I realized I had experienced grief for the first time in my life, but it was definitely from a retrospective perspective. I had this epiphany as I prepared to write my first book, *From Pieces to Peace*, in April 2018. The main focus of that book was to shine the light on traumas I had experienced throughout the earlier part of my life. While I was writing from a healed place, the primary goal of the book was to help others heal, be delivered, and restored from the traumas that many people experience but rarely speak of. Though many parts of delivering that message were hard, I confidently addressed every trauma relevant to the cause.

From the loss of my maternal grandmother, abuse, addiction, and molestation, I peeled back the layers of the grief my traumas had caused as if I were a butterfly shedding a cocoon.

These traumas had an even more extreme impact on my life because the initial trauma and grief of it all was never properly addressed. This is mainly due to the fact that I either suffered in silence, hid from my truth, or in my naivety, failed to realize the impact that the occurrences made on the way I went about life in the future. Once I became aware of how I responded to trauma and navigated the grief process, I became intentional about my healing journey. Somewhere between deliverance and new traumas, I got lost. Lost in limbo between I'm okay and I'm not okay. This alone has made it virtually impossible for me to take direct action toward my own healing over the past twelve months. My struggle with holding on to my emotional status of being okay was more rooted in the fear that I had never been healed and delivered in the first place. My time in denial far outweighed my brief moments of acceptance.

The fact of the matter is that life had happened to me, which meant I had NEW things to heal and deliver from. Hence, "infinite healing." This has been my greatest revelation about my own healing to date. People often reference the metamorphosis of a butterfly when it comes to healing and transformation. The metamorphosis of a butterfly is one of life's great wonders and a symbol of one of the most beautiful processes in life—healing and transformation. The transformation of a butterfly begins with the female butterfly. Once she mates with a male butterfly, she lays approximately 1,000 eggs and then dies. However, the new eggs make a beautiful transformation from egg to caterpillar, cocoon, and then a beautiful new butterfly. The pain in the process is the death of the male butterfly after mating and the death of the female butterfly after laying the eggs.

Where I personally got it wrong and what led me to my most recent stagnant state in the grieving process is that I focused on the fact that I had already made the transition. I believed my most painful healing journey had come to an end because I transitioned from the egg to the butterfly after healing from a mountain of trauma. I was so attached to my butterfly stage that I missed several opportunities to experience metamorphosis and heal again. As life happens and new traumas arise, it is important to release your butterfly stage. Allow that season of your life to come to an end and be okay with evolving through a new metamorphosis journey. The

17

metamorphosis of a butterfly to me is one of the most beautiful symbols of the healing and transformation process, a process that begins with pain or the death of the beautifully healed butterfly, and never truly ends. With each transition of a butterfly, it is important to recognize the new opportunity—the eggs!

In December 2019, I began experiencing feelings of confusion, anger, and exhaustion, but it wasn't until September 2020 when I realized I had met my end. But why? How did I somehow unearth such painful grief out of nowhere? I didn't. It had been there, in me and on me, buried under my super-spiritual beliefs and values since I experienced the first new trauma in early 2018. I was so focused on holding on to my previous healing so tight I did not realize it was time to release what was dead and look forward to the new transformation and healing to come. Over the span of two years, I had again experienced unsurmountable traumas that had reaccumulated since my last transformation. These traumas were magnified by the most recent events of 2020: Covid-19, being diagnosed with Chiari Malformation, having a house fire, being displaced from my home for three months, and losing my job. It became clearer as time progressed, that the healing I was gripping so tightly was causing more and more pain. I had been flying high since healing a lifetime of old wounds, but by this time, I had experienced new trauma, and I failed to acknowledge the fact that I was experiencing the grieving process from traumas that dated back to January 2018. From infidelity that I had forgiven, to being held accountable for the decision I made that affected my entire family...the list goes on. My initial acknowledgment of my feelings in December came on the heels of my husband's return from being stationed overseas for a year. While I anxiously awaited his return at the end of 2019, I had no idea of the trauma many of us would experience in 2020.

At the onset of 2020, the world encountered a pandemic that would not only expose the entire world to grief, but it also left us with limited resources and outlets to transition through it. From experiencing the trauma of loss due to the Coronavirus outbreak to being isolated from family and friends for months upon months, we were essentially left to virtually find our own way to process and heal. The pandemic forced most of the world to sit still, left to deal with all of the things we had neglected for months—for many of us, years! From personal care, deep cleaning, and sprucing up our homes, to sprucing up our minds and overall emotional well-being, the Coronavirus magnified our individual emotions quotient in how

19

we respond to trauma. While it revealed many emotional strengths and weaknesses globally, it exposed the brokenness of my family and my career instability, and I completely failed to cope. Some of us experienced variable levels of depression that went unaddressed, myself included, while others recognized grief earlier on and sought out the support of therapists, family, spiritual leaders, and friends to help cope with the effects of the pandemic. By the end of the year, I think we all realized the Coronavirus pandemic was not going to be a fly by night occurrence but one that would create many life-altering circumstances.

One thing I would like to make clear is not everyone will experience grief in the same way. Some will numb through it as I have for far too long, while others will be intentional about getting through the process. The cornerstone of healing through grief is to acknowledge the trauma and its impact on your life, become self-aware of how you respond to trauma, and make the decision to heal intentionally. Regardless of how you were affected by grief, know there is hope. Release your butterfly and have hope in knowing you now have the opportunity to experience a new transition, the metamorphosis from egg to an even more beautifully refined butterfly.

## AFFIRMATIONS

Write the affirmations in the space provided
below and recite it aloud as often as you need.

# *I COMMIT TO MY HEALING.*

# *I WILL GET THROUGH THIS.*

# I AM STRONGER THAN MY GRIEF.

---

---

---

---

---

# I AM COURAGEOUS.

---

---

---

---

---

---

---

---

---

---

---

## A DEEPER LOOK

How has the pandemic contributed to your grief?

_____

_____

_____

_____

_____

_____

_____

_____

_____

_____

_____

_____

_____

_____

23

What are some positive things that happened in your life during 2020?

_____

_____

_____

_____

_____

_____

_____

_____

_____

_____

_____

_____

_____

_____

_____

# RELEASE

Freely express your overall emotions below.

_____

_____

_____

_____

_____

_____

_____

_____

_____

_____

_____

_____

_____

_____

# PART II

# RECOGNIZING GRIEF

## LIFE VS. GRIEF

Are you having a "no good, very bad day", or are you experiencing grief? We all have our good and bad days but is it just a bad day or should you consider the idea that you are truly experiencing grief. Having a bad day or bad week does not automatically equate to being depressed; and being depressed does not automatically equate to having a lifetime diagnosis of mental illness. What triggered your negative or inconsistent emotions? How did you respond when you became aware of the trigger? These are important questions to ask yourself in order to identify and address grief, especially for the purpose of seeking intentional healing.

The journey of life can and will throw us a barrage of curveballs in the form of trauma, but how do we respond? Whether we intentionally choose to respond or not, it is important to note the way we respond will determine the outcome and roadmap to our healing. Do you respond with negative emotions such as denial, anger, fear, or isolation? Or do you have a more positive response such as self-love, self-care, and self-preservation? The way you respond will determine your overall experience throughout the grieving process. Does that mean that people with a positive response will have a painless expeditious healing process? Absolutely not! Pain is an unfortunate part of the process. Choosing to heal intentionally versus dwelling on the negative aspects of the trauma that caused you to grieve in the first place can certainly make the process easier. Responding positively more often than negatively will produce more beneficial outcomes throughout the process.

You must first be willing to be honest with yourself regarding what you have experienced and how you either consciously or subconsciously respond in order to recognize grief. Acknowledging the specific trauma that happened to you is vital! Simply ignoring the specific trauma can not only be detrimental, but it will also contribute to the length of your healing process. This is where I not only got it wrong, but I also caused my process to be longer and more painful by simply acting like the trauma did not exist. I spent time downplaying things with the silent hope that they would just go away and be replaced with good circumstances, feelings, and outcomes. Let's face it, it is far better and emotionally healthy to address one trauma versus trying to do as I've had to do and peel back layers of trauma on top of layers of trauma long after the fact. This has been the source of so much unnecessary pain for me. One earth-shattering, life-altering trauma that I experienced was being molested as a child. I cannot tell you my initial trauma response because I was too young to remember, but I do remember having a bedwetting problem during my early adolescent years. While as a child, I had no control over how to cope with such a devastating trauma; it still left a lasting impression on me as I attempted to navigate my teenage and early adulthood years. As I matured as an adult, mid-twenties, I realized that the trauma I first experienced as a four- or five-year-old was an experience that was at the forefront of my emotional responses and well-being for over twenty years later.

I eventually realized I had experienced trauma. Unfortunately for me, though, by that time, the first trauma had snowballed into a multitude of traumas that consistently went unaddressed. Grief had been a part of my entire life, and while I was unaware, it showed up in who I was at the time. I wasn't living the life I wanted, I was simply living the life that was given to me in the form of trauma, grief, heartache, and bad, very bad decisions. I was angry and bitter with most everyone and everything in my life, often resulting in isolation, helplessness, and eventually, numbness. I stuffed the trauma so deep that when I was triggered by a similar circumstance or a new traumatic experience, I responded on the extremely negative spectrum of grief with anger, rage, suicidal ideation, and depression. I had become a product of unaddressed trauma, which led me to make bad choices and treat people poorly resulting in more trauma, devastation, and heartache. It was a vicious cycle of the well-known cliché that "hurt people, hurt people." The hurt I experienced as a child had manifested into years of me hurting others intentionally and unintentionally.

The onset of grief can produce feelings that you may recognize immediately, but due to the shock of it all, it may take days, weeks, months, and even years to become aware of the fact that you are or have been experiencing grief. One of the best ways to recognize whether you are experiencing grief is to first become self-aware. Are you aware of how you typically respond to stress, anxiety, and trauma? Do you self-isolate, lash out, or busy yourself to mask the pain? While these are a few natural responses, there are so many more to consider such as decreased self-esteem, changes in appetite, sleeplessness, difficulty concentrating, excessive drinking, substance abuse, partying, and paranoia, to name a few. When you are self-aware, you are more inclined to have a "this is not me" epiphany and realize something is not right with your mental and emotional well-being.

In December 2018, I recognized who I knew myself to be was aggressively eroding away, but I fought tirelessly to maintain the parts of me that were still there. I was in limbo between this is me—denial, and this is not me—acceptance. Like a hamster on a wheel going nowhere, fighting to hold on to the things I believed were a part of my identity, refusing to lose...but I lost me and everything that I was holding on to in the process. This is why self-awareness and self-preservation are important. When you're in an emotional space that just doesn't feel right, be courageous enough to trust your gut, take action, and address it immediately. No one knows you, like you! Doing so will aid in self-preservation and protecting yourself from unnecessary grief and pain.

If you have not reached the point in your journey where you feel you are well enough acquainted with yourself to recognize that something is not right with you, that's okay, for now. That does not mean you will not be able to recognize you are grieving. It just means you need to be intentional in getting to know who you are. Who is at the core of your being? Not the tangible or material things that are apart of you, such as your marital, social, or career status. What does your soul say about you aside from the tangible and material things? What pleases your soul? What doesn't? The thing about life is that we often experience metamorphosis as we mature; experience trauma or change in general. I am personally still learning things about myself as I mature with experience. Learning what I like, dislike, how I respond to life, and what truly triggers me has been a journey in and of itself. These learning experiences have been helping me to cope with trauma and navigate grief as it comes.

Taking the time to really acknowledge your current and transitioning feelings is key. Instead of settling with simply being angry, be brave enough to go deeper and question why you are experiencing that emotion. When questioning why you are experiencing that emotion, take care in avoiding blame-shifting and deflecting. Focus on questions like, "Why am I angry?" "What triggered this response?" "What part did I play?" The more you question your emotional responses, the clearer you will become on how you truly feel. Recognizing and acknowledging your true feelings will clarify your path toward intentional healing.

## AFFIRMATIONS

Write the affirmations in the space provided
below and recite it aloud as often as you need.

# I CHOOSE LIFE.

_____

_____

_____

_____

_____

# I RELEASE THE TENSION IN MY BODY AND RELAX.

_____

_____

_____

_____

_____

# I WILL TAKE THE TIME TO CARE FOR MY NEEDS TODAY.

_____

_____

_____

_____

_____

_____

# I CHOOSE TO HEAL GRACEFULLY.

_____

_____

_____

_____

_____

_____

## A DEEPER LOOK

Do you have the life you desire? Why or why not?

_____

_____

_____

_____

_____

_____

_____

_____

_____

_____

_____

_____

_____

_____

_____

35

What is your natural response to trauma?

_____

_____

_____

_____

_____

_____

_____

_____

_____

_____

_____

_____

_____

_____

_____

What are your triggers?

_____

_____

_____

_____

_____

_____

_____

_____

_____

_____

_____

_____

_____

_____

_____

_____

_____

## **RELEASE**

Freely describe the life you envision for yourself in the future.

_____

_____

_____

_____

_____

_____

_____

_____

_____

_____

_____

_____

_____

_____

## UNPREDICTABLE GRIEF

Grief is such an unpredictable journey that we all experience, and in many cases, there are some grievances that we will never "just get over." Especially when it comes to a traumatic experience such as the loss of a loved one. We may learn to cope with the loss but not completely "get over" the reality that the loved one is no longer a part of our lives. That is an unfortunate truth that we must be willing to accept in an attempt to cope throughout the grieving process. The fact that we may not just get over it doesn't mean we are incapable of healing, nor does it mean we are required to sulk in sadness for the rest of our lives. What it means is, it is okay to feel through the emotions that grief produces without completely forgetting the trauma that led you there.

There are a myriad of opinions and case studies that identify grief as stages, phases, or cycles. My goal, however, is to shed light on the fact that while grief is a process that does indeed come in stages, phases, and cycles, there is no order or rule defining which emotional response you will experience or when you will experience it. You can bounce back and forth between multiple emotions, sometimes only experiencing a few and in nonsequential order. You can experience anger, deep sadness, even joy, and then bounce back to the space of anger and resentment within a matter of days before you even reach the point of healing through grief. That's okay! Know that experiencing multiple types of negative emotions even after you think you've transitioned to a healthier, more positive emotional state is completely normal. Whether you experience a few emotions or many, acknowledging and addressing these emotions still contributes to your healing process.

Shock, denial, pain, guilt, anger, bargaining, and depression are some of the most grievous trauma response emotions (phases) that you may experience. Do not feel ashamed, displaced, or embarrassed by your emotions? They are natural human responses. What is most important is that you take the time to feel. Instead of masking the pain of it all, let it burn! For me, when I initially experience trauma within my marriage, I was not only in total shock and disbelief, but I also spent a large amount of time telling myself I was okay. The timing could not have been worse. Mentally and emotionally, I was in a place where I was experiencing so many changes within my personal life that I desperately NEEDED to be okay. But I wasn't, not by far. What I needed was to face it, see it for what it was and had the potential to become if I did not address it. I needed to acknowledge the situations that led to my emotional instability, take the time to feel, and process my emotions appropriately. Masking and avoiding dealing with myself only stagnated and complicated my healing process.

In being intentional during your journey, let me encourage you for a moment with a very true and impactful cliché, "It's okay to not be okay." With intentional healing, not only will you be okay, but you will also come out of this process as a better version of yourself. Refined, stronger, wiser, and with a deeper understanding of who you are, not just who you have the potential to be. Many times, healed people turn the pain of their grief into purpose that will help someone else to heal through similar circumstances. The possibilities of how you will come out on the other side are endless. DO NOT rush the process! Take the time and put in the effort to pay attention to your emotions and how you process them. Lack of attention to your emotional well-being can cause you to stay in one specific emotional stage far too long, which also stifles your process. I encourage you to take the time to FEEL but do not sit and wallow in those negative feelings. Know that your feelings and emotions are valid regardless of what anyone else thinks, but they are not the sum total of who you are and who you are to become.

Your process is your process and yours alone. You are the only human being responsible for your healing. Once you become aware that you are experiencing grief, it is your responsibility to heal intentionally. Waiting for grief to "just pass" will not assist you in the process, it will only slow you down or stop you in your tracks, affecting the way you function as a human being in every area of your life. It takes intentional work on your end. Healing, hope, and acceptance are the positive trauma responses necessary for overcoming the grief process, which we will discuss in greater detail. But for now, let's identify where you are in your journey.

## AFFIRMATIONS

Write the affirmations in the space provided
below and recite it aloud as often as you need.

# I AM SELF-AWARE.

_____

_____

_____

_____

_____

# I CAN COPE WITH THE
# GRIEVING PROCESS.

_____

_____

_____

_____

_____

# I GIVE MYSELF TIME AND SPACE TO FEEL ALL OF MY FEELINGS.

---

---

---

---

# I RECOGNIZE PAINFUL MOMENTS, BUT I KNOW THEY WILL PASS.

---

---

---

---

## A DEEPER LOOK

What emotion(s) are you currently feeling? Are you experiencing more negative emotions such as anger, denial, shock, or depression?

_____

_____

_____

_____

_____

_____

_____

_____

_____

_____

_____

_____

_____

_____

_____

_____

Once you identify your current emotions, identify how you are coping? Are you sleeping more or less, eating more or less, emotionally numb, or lashing out?

_____

_____

_____

_____

_____

_____

_____

_____

_____

_____

_____

_____

_____

_____

_____

_____

_____

## **RELEASE**

Freely describe the emotions you need to feel again. These emotions will help foster your healing journey.

_____

_____

_____

_____

_____

_____

_____

_____

_____

_____

_____

_____

_____

_____

_____

# PART III

# OVERCOMING

## GRADUAL HEALING

Let's face it. We all want the product of healing, but we don't want to experience the pain of it all. I wish I could tell you the healing process will be swift and painless; unfortunately, that is just not the case. There will be times of joy, pain, confusion, comfort, sadness, and peace. What is most important is making the cognizant decision to heal intentionally and trust that you will heal in your own time. In all honesty, at least this has been true for me and other people in my life, sometimes our negative emotions feel much more comfortable, so we hide behind them. This is especially when those emotions are justified by the trauma you've experienced; however, because it feels better does not mean it is better for you. I have come to learn that we experience growth and healing often in some of the most uncomfortable places and under the most uncomfortable circumstances. Our outcome is primarily based on our actions and responses as we navigate the healing process.

Is it possible to just "wing it" during the healing process? Absolutely! But intentional healing requires intentional planning and actions to move forward. Once you make the decision you are ready to deal with your mess and heal, it is important to determine how. How will you manage your emotions? How will you respond to negative consequences or circumstances as you seek to heal?

The key to effectively managing your emotions is to see them for what they are and respond appropriately. If you're angry, go deeper and question why. Once you identify the emotions you are experiencing and take the time to feel, you must be willing to take action and replace the negative emotions with positive emotions and actions. That means if your norm is sleeping all day while you are grieving, implement some self-care actions such as exercising or taking a drive to the lake to relax. If your norm is responding to stress and anxiety with lashing out, consider implementing meditation, prayer, or journaling. These are just a few examples of replacing negative responses with positive ones. Choose to replace your negative responses with positive, life-giving things that you enjoy. If you are in a phase of your life where you are discovering or re-discovering yourself, this is a perfect time to begin a new hobby, try things you've never tried before, or revisit something you had not done in a long time that brings you joy. This time for me, I chose to do a complete soul detox. This consisted of addressing every weight that I had been carrying over the past year without the interference of outside influences. To add to it, I made time to take a trip home (Ohio and Michigan) to spend extended time with family without distractions. No social media or over-stimulating social events. I spent the time being loved well by family and just being...without worry. As you replace these negative responses with positive actions, you will find that your overall mood will be elevated. You will feel lighter and clearer about taking the next steps toward healing, whether that means making some life changes, seeing a therapist, or confronting your trauma. Now, I am not saying that as soon as you begin adding positive action you won't feel the need to fall back into your old, more comfortable, and negative habits. But as you take the time to implement new habits, the old ones will feel less comfortable.

Gradual healing requires seeking intentional discomfort. This may come as a surprise coming from me, someone who has often been referred to as "churchy," but here it goes.

"Church" is not meant to replace therapy. This is especially when addressing healing through the grief process. While prayer/spiritual healing is an important part of our daily lives, not only is it okay to see a therapist/licensed professional counselor (LPC), I also firmly recommend it. Neither is meant to replace the other, but I encourage you to implement BOTH spiritual and professional support into your healing journey. Granted, it is never comfortable to sit alone with a stranger and bare your soul, well, not for most of us, but it is a necessary discomfort that I recommend you seek if you are struggling with identifying ways to heal. Spiritual healing is almost often expected to be a one-stop-shop for healing from grief, but think of it this way, our God has given the professional counseling community the gift of understanding the human psyche for the purpose of healing. While you will do the majority of the work, a LPC can help you process your feelings and help you to better navigate the grieving process and learn things about yourself, such as what your triggers and responses are and why. That is their purpose.

The healing journey does not look the same for everyone. What's amazing is that while many of the symptoms of the grieving process can be unpredictable, you still have the power to control your narrative. It is your responsibility to at least implement a plan for your healing journey. I will be the first to admit that clearly defining a plan for my process proved to be difficult. This was not something I could effectively navigate on my own, so in developing a safe support system, I was intentional about soliciting the help of a therapist to take this journey with me. During our first session, we went DEEP, despite the fact that during the entire drive to his office I kept thinking to myself, "Robin, keep it light...just get a little acquainted." As we surpassed making acquaintances and worked toward setting goals and creating an action plan, he looked up from his MacBook where he had been taking notes and said, "You have to control the narrative." I can't lie, I felt some type of way because I was more than certain I was in control of everything, especially the narrative. But just as I began to defend, he very calmly repeated before I could get the words out, "You have to control the narrative." That's when it hit me! My perspective had been so tainted by grief that I had spent too much time in a reactive, defensive state versus a proactive, offensive one. It was that day that my healing plan had been activated, and I gained more clarity as to what to do next.

Just as your symptoms can be unpredictable, your journey, even with goals and plans, will not be a straight and narrow path. There will be mountains to climb and valleys to overcome, but one thing is for sure, you will get through this and come out on the other side stronger, wiser, and much better than you were prior to your encounter with grief. So, don't count yourself out. You have a choice. You can either allow life to happen to you or participate in creating the life you desire by seeking intentional healing. It is often natural to feel like a victim to your circumstances, but in essence, the longer you subscribe to the victim mindset, the more you rehearse the pain and re-live the trauma. Re-living your trauma stagnates your healing process and deepens the emotional wounds that trauma created. Instead of repeating over and over what happened to you, spend that time and energy renewing your mind and creating a plan to truly overcome your circumstances and emotions.

## AFFIRMATIONS

Write the affirmations in the space provided
below and recite it aloud as often as you need.

# *I HAVE A LIFE BEYOND MY TRAUMA.*

_____

_____

_____

_____

# *I WILL HOLD ON TO LOVE AND RELEASE THE GRIEF.*

_____

_____

_____

_____

_____

# I CHOOSE TO FEEL THE PRESENCE AND LOVE OF MY FAMILY AND FRIENDS.

_____

_____

_____

_____

_____

# I CHOOSE TO PARTICIPATE IN CREATING THE LIFE I WANT TO LIVE.

_____

_____

_____

_____

_____

_____

## A DEEPER LOOK

What story are you telling yourself and others?

How can you change the narrative of your story (life)?

_____

_____

_____

_____

_____

_____

_____

_____

_____

_____

_____

_____

_____

_____

## RELEASE

Freely describe your plan for intentional healing.

_____

_____

_____

_____

_____

_____

_____

_____

_____

_____

_____

_____

_____

_____

_____

## HEAL AND FORGIVE, BUT REMEMBER

Healing, hope, and acceptance are three of the most positive and pivotal stages of the grief process. The way I see it, hope and acceptance are the catalysts that foster the healing journey. Hope for a better tomorrow and hope for a true change in your circumstances are example thoughts that help you move toward acceptance. Once you see the situation for what it is or isn't, it is much easier to find hope for what is to come as a part of your healing transformation. There are times when you feel the need to justify your actions and emotions, so you re-live the trauma by repeating or reaffirming the occurrence. Do not be consumed by feeling the need to justify your emotions. Know that your feelings are valid, and no one can validate your emotions but you.

Guilt can keep us from experiencing hope right away. It is very easy to get stuck in the place of guilt, shame, and even fear of condemnation, but none of those emotions are healthy or conducive to your healing. A lot of times, we stand in guilt because we have yet to seek or extend forgiveness. Forgiveness is the major key to freedom from guilt, shame, and condemnation. Lack of forgiveness, though, can keep you bound to these negative emotions regardless of who was right, wrong, or misunderstood.

Once you're courageously forgiven and extended forgiveness, have hope to overcome grief, become a better you, or even hope to gain in some way through healing. I understand that there are times where we hope that the circumstance had not happened, but how does that contribute to your healing? We cannot change the past, but we definitely have the ability to choose our thoughts toward the future. The more we foster positive thoughts and emotions toward ourselves and our circumstances, the easier it is to accept and overcome them.

Choosing to forgive and seek forgiveness can be an unnerving process. There were many traumas I experienced within the last year that left me completely shattered! I found myself feeling hypocritical because I felt like the offenses that led up to the trauma were unforgivable. I had no intentions of seeking or extending forgiveness. They hurt me, and I was done with them! I now realize that while that was a natural trauma response, it is not the positive response that is required to foster growth. Even in the unforgivable, there was still a requirement for me to seek AND extend forgiveness, even in the worst cases. Accepting the fact that it is okay to forgive the offense and remember the impact of the trauma was the catalyst to my renewed mindset and willingness to forgive and remember, as well as seek forgiveness without expectation. Ultimately, I had to release myself and the offenders from my unforgiveness and just let it be.

Forgiving and remembering is a precautionary method necessary to avoid repeating the same cycles of trauma that I, too, played a part in based on my own choices. The cycles of heartache, betrayal, and being mishandled are not new to me. In fact, they are cycles I have experienced in different ways because I failed to make the right choices, forgive, heal, and remember. I encourage you to forgive yourself and others, as well as release the offense and the hurt, but remember.

## AFFIRMATIONS

Write the affirmations in the space provided below and recite it aloud as often as you need.

# I AM FULLY PRESENT IN THIS MOMENT.

_____

_____

_____

_____

# I RELEASE GUILT AND ACCEPT FORGIVENESS.

_____

_____

_____

_____

# I HAVE CONTROL OF MY EMOTIONS.

_____

_____

_____

_____

# MY FEELINGS ARE VALID.

_____

_____

_____

# I AM SAFE AND I AM LOVED.

_____

_____

_____

_____

THE METAMORPHOSIS OF A GRIEVING SOUL

## **A DEEPER LOOK**

What are you struggling to accept?

_____

_____

_____

_____

_____

_____

_____

_____

_____

_____

_____

_____

_____

_____

Will you consider seeing a Licensed Professional Counselor when you experience grief? Why, or why not?

_____

_____

_____

_____

_____

_____

_____

_____

_____

_____

_____

_____

_____

_____

_____

_____

What positive feelings and emotions will you intentionally implement to replace the negative ones?

_____

_____

_____

_____

_____

_____

_____

_____

_____

_____

_____

_____

_____

_____

# **RELEASE**

Write a letter of forgiveness to yourself and write one to the person(s) involved in your trauma.

_____

_____

_____

_____

_____

_____

_____

_____

_____

_____

_____

_____

_____

_____

# *PART IV*

# *THRIVE*

## BRAND NEW ME!

Trauma and grief have a way of either changing us for the better and for the worst. Failure to truly overcome grief, leads you down a slippery slope toward experiencing a similar trauma, which will lead to re-entering the grieving process. This can be from a failure to cope altogether or failure to be honest with yourself and accept the circumstance for what it is. My hope for you reading this is that you come out on the other side of this as a precious diamond: refined, renewed, resilient, and optimistic.

Life as you had come to know it has changed because of the traumatic experiences that have occurred in your life. Will you choose to accept what is and move forward? Having a positive perspective as you heal has proven to be the best way to really get to know and embrace your new life—the new you! It has been my experience that I have lost parts of myself through grief, but gratefully I was able to discover new parts of myself that better served me during this new season of life. Sometimes when we experience grief, it truly reveals how attached we have been to things like jobs, relationships, loved ones, and even material things. These attachments are all seemingly harmless and healthy until we lose them. Now, pause. Am I saying that it is wrong to love your job, friends, partner, or things like your car? No, not at all. But losing them reveals how truly attached we were to them. Giving yourself permission to release these things is courageous, and it also helps you lighten the emotional baggage that you carry with you into your next phase of life.

I personally have had the experience of losing every last one of these things. To say the least, the process of healing was ugly every single time, and sometimes experiencing a combination of losses at once. However, I can attest to the fact that I realized how some of these attachments were not only unhealthy, but they also caused me to lose sight of who I truly was. I had to re-learn who Robin was, and create new norms, beliefs, and change the way I managed relationships and my attachment to things moving forward. No longer am I the girl with over 200 pairs of shoes and clothes I never wear because I'm too afraid to detach from them. No longer do I spend my life managing everyone else's emotions, needs, and expectations while neglecting my own. While I live life as a giver and servant of others, I ensure I am good first. I tend to my mental, physical, and emotional needs first to avoid emptying myself on account of a job, friend, partner, family member, or client, leaving nothing for myself in the end. This came with healing and truly getting to know me better.

Getting to know yourself through the healing process is something that you will indeed experience, whether intentionally or unintentionally. So why not take the time to foster growth and self-awareness intentionally. Step outside of your comfort zone. If you're always in the house watching TV or scrolling social media, perhaps try taking a walk in your neighborhood, at the park, or another more scenic area. If you're suffering from the devastation of losing your job, and that is all you know when it comes to life, consider trying out a different industry or even starting your own business. You will never know what you truly enjoy in life or what you are good at until you try doing things you have never done before. From new foods to jobs, hobbies, and your dating preferences, how will you discover new parts of yourself if you never step outside of your comfort zone? Whatever you choose to do, remember you have the power to control your narrative. Be courageous enough to thrive in the midst of your infinite healing journey regardless of what it looks like today.

I desperately wish that I could tell you I have arrived at my transformation destination, but I can't. The truth is that my metamorphosis is only just beginning. I am transitioning from the egg to the caterpillar and am looking forward to graceful healing in this season...in spite of. What I will share with you, though, is that God has a funny way of ensuring that we grow through the very thing that he places on our hearts for the purpose of healing others. Prior to acknowledging my own struggles with grief, this book had already been written with those who were affected by "Covid-19 grief" in mind. But I couldn't release it. Despite the fact that the manuscript had been completed for months, my spirit kept saying, "not yet." I'm so grateful that I obediently waited. I did not know it at the time, but the wait was solely for the purpose of pouring more of myself into these pages to help you to know you are not alone. I am transitioning with you. Healed people heal people. So, as you embark on your healing journey, be intentional in leading the next person toward infinite healing.

## AFFIRMATIONS

Write the affirmations in the space provided
below and recite it aloud as often as you need.

# *I WILL HOLD ON TO LOVE AND RELEASE THE GRIEF.*

_____

_____

_____

_____

# *I WILL TAKE THE TIME TO CARE FOR MY NEEDS TODAY.*

_____

_____

_____

_____

# *I CHOOSE TO FEEL AT PEACE TODAY.*

---

---

---

---

---

# *I COMMIT TO INFINITE HEALING.*

---

---

---

---

---

## A DEEPER LOOK

How will you intentionally learn new things about yourself?

_____

_____

_____

_____

_____

_____

_____

_____

_____

_____

_____

_____

_____

_____

What have you learned about yourself so far?

_____

_____

_____

_____

_____

_____

_____

_____

_____

_____

_____

_____

_____

_____

_____

_____

_____

## **RELEASE**

Write an affirmation statement affirming who you are, where you see yourself in the future, and your declaration of healing.

_____

_____

_____

_____

_____

_____

_____

_____

_____

_____

_____

_____

_____

_____

_____

## ACKNOWLEDGMENTS

What a journey this transition toward transformation has been, and it is not nearly over yet! I thank God for his covering as I navigate trauma, disappointment, and grief. Despite my disobedience, frustration, and sheer inability to keep my faith strong, God has kept me, comforted, and provided for me. He was strategic in sending me the support system of old friends, and solid family, when I needed them most.

Mariah and Diamond, no words can express my gratitude for you! From relocations, to adapting to change, and even trauma-drama, you two have been so resilient, supportive, and mature over the years. You have been amazing daughters, actually the BEST DAUGHTERS a mother could ask for. Thank you for giving me the space to heal and grow as I continue to navigate motherhood. I love you two infinitely.

To my parents, thank you so much for everything you are, and everything you do. I never saw myself needing something as simple as a hug, prayer, or just your presence more than I had during the toughest days of my life, but you were always there.

A'Maya (Baby Sis), thank you for allowing me the space to be a sister; sometimes sister-mom (LOL), and friend. The time we spend together last year gave me a greater appreciation for our relationship and bond. I LOVE and MISS YOU SO MUCH!!!

My siblings (Da Sibs), thank you for the many laughs, fun times, and love! You all may not have known that I was struggling but it didn't matter because you were there when I needed you.

Ma'Kieta, my boo! You have been such a bright light! Your wisdom, support, honesty, and sheer ability to make me laugh every time we speak is amazing! Thank you, you truly are someone that I'm sure will be stuck with me for the rest of this lifetime! I love you.

To my sister-friends Denelle, Sherhonda, Stephanie R., Stephanie H.(cousin), Atasha (cousin), Teena and Erin, the hardest part about living miles apart, is not being able to just come sit on your couch, chit-chat, laugh, eat and just breath. Somehow, each and every single one of you made that possible at some point during this journey and I appreciate it more than you know! Who's planning the next girls trip cause I'm ready yesterday (LOL)! I love you all!

Trena aka Sister-BooBae 2.0, I cannot thank you enough for the sisterhood we have cultivated over these past two years! I know one thing, if don't nobody else pray for me, my SBB 2.0 def will!

81

Your prayers and encouraging words were always felt whether I expressed it enough or not. I love you and am grateful to consider you my forever friend.

Shawn, ha! I can now say that you've seen the best more professional side of me and the cray-cray, vulnerable side of me and I am ok with that (LOL). God has a way of sending the most unexpected people to speak life and wisdom into you, without judgement or condemnation. You truly are a godsend. I am grateful for your business partnership and the privilege of calling you a trusted friend. I love you!

Syreeia, we have known of one another for a few years now but didn't really get to know one another until late 2020. Thank you for your obedience, what you meant to be a business connection, God ordained to be a divine connection.

Just as importantly, a huge thank you to the POWER TRIBE! My readers, editor, graphic artists, clients, and customers! I know many of you may not have known that I was experiencing grief, but each of you have been the glue that has held me together during some of my silent and rough days. Thank you. I love and appreciate you all, maybe more than you'll ever know

-Robin Major-Oliphant

## BOOKS FROM THE AUTHOR

**From Pieces to Peace:** *Damaged Goods*
(Available on Amazon and Kindle)

**From Pieces to Peace:** *Forgiving the Unforgivable*
(Available on Amazon and Kindle)

**Freedom Through Forgiveness** *an Interactive Journal and Daily Devotional*
(Available on Amazon)

**Love You:** *Unconditionally an Anthology*
(Available on Amazon and Kindle)

**Memoirs of Military Wives** *an Anthology*
(Available on Amazon and Kindle)

**Unconditional Submission**
(Available on Amazon and Kindle)

**It Is Finished**: *The First Time Author's Guide to Completing Your Manuscript*
(Available on Amazon)

**Infinite Healing:** *The Metamorphosis of a Grieving Soul*
(Available on Amazon)

Made in the USA
Monee, IL
16 February 2021